cookies & bars

cookies & bars

mouthwatering cookie sheet treats

Cover design by Andrew Easton @ Ummagumma

ISBN: 978-1-4454-0672-5

Printed in China

Notes for the Reader

This book uses imperial, metric, or US cup measurements. Follow the same units of measurement throughout; do not mix imperial and metric. All spoon measurements are level: teaspoons are assumed to be 5 ml, and tablespoons are assumed to be 15 ml. Unless otherwise stated, milk is assumed to be whole, eggs and individual vegetables such as potatoes are medium, and pepper is freshly ground black pepper. Recipes using raw or very lightly cooked eggs should be avoided by infants, the elderly, pregnant women, convalescents, and anyone suffering from an illness.

contents

Introduction

THERE IS NOTHING TO MATCH THE INIMITABLE FLAVOR OF A COOKIE THAT HAS BEEN FRESHLY BAKED THAT DAY. BAKING COOKIES IN YOUR OWN KITCHEN IS IMMENSELY SATISFYING (IN FACT, SOME DON'T EVEN REQUIRE BAKING). IN ADDITION, THEY'RE EASY TO MAKE AND TAKE VERY LITTLE TIME, SO YOU CAN WHISK UP A BATCH OF TASTY TREATS IN NO TIME AT ALL. YOU CAN EVEN ENCOURAGE THE KIDS—MAJOR CONSUMERS OF COOKIES AND BARS, AFTER ALL—TO HELP MIX THE DOUGH AND CUT IT OUT. THIS COULD BE A CONSTRUCTIVE AND FUN RAINY DAY PASTIME.

The recipes in this book are divided into four chapters. The first three feature chocolate, fruit, and nuts,

while the fourth offers more elegant cookies for special occasions and, perhaps, for gifts to family and friends.

Among all these cookies and bars you are sure to find at least one that is perfect for morning coffee, afternoon

tea, school lunch boxes, filling the after-school gap, or serving with ice cream for dessert. From family

favorites, such as brownies and oat-style cookies, to delicate morsels, such as florentines and amaretti, you

will be spoiled for choice.

Perennially popular with adults and children alike, chocolate cookies, brownies, and bars are, arguably, everybody's favorite sweet treat. Certainly, chocoholics will not be disappointed by the fabulous collection of recipes in this chapter, which includes everything from what might be described as the best cookies in the world—Double Chocolate Chip Cookies—to mouthwatering Caramel Chocolate Shortbread.

Cooking with chocolate is not difficult, but it does require a little care. To blend chocolate with other ingredients, it usually needs to be melted. The easiest way to do this is to break it into small pieces and place in a heatproof bowl. Set the bowl over a pan of gently simmering, not boiling, water and heat until the chocolate has melted. Do not let the bottom of the bowl touch the

CHOCOLATE HEAVEN

surface of the water and make sure that, if you are stirring the chocolate or a mixture of chocolate and other ingredients, water does not splash into the bowl. This will make the chocolate grainy and spoil the texture of the cookie or its chocolate topping. You can also melt chocolate in the microwave. Break it into pieces and arrange in a microwave dish. Check with the manufacturer's handbook for timings, bearing in mind that white chocolate should be melted on medium, while dark or milk chocolate can be melted on high. Remove the dish and stir frequently to check whether the chocolate has melted—it may not look as if it has. Chocolate can be melted over direct heat in a pan if it is combined with one or more other ingredients, such as butter and syrup.

MAKES 24

1 stick unsalted butter, softened,
    plus extra for greasing
generous ¼ cup golden granulated
    sugar
generous ¼ cup light muscovado
    sugar

1 egg, beaten
½ tsp vanilla extract
generous ¾ cup all-purpose flour
2 tbsp unsweetened cocoa
½ tsp baking soda
⅔ cup milk chocolate chips
½ cup walnuts, coarsely chopped

Double Chocolate Chip Cookies

The minimum cooking time will produce cookies that are soft and chewy in the middle. The longer cooking time will result in crisper cookies.

• Preheat the oven to 350°F/180°C, then grease 3 cookie sheets. Place the butter, granulated sugar, and muscovado sugar in a bowl and beat until light and fluffy. Gradually beat in the egg and vanilla extract.

• Sift the flour, cocoa, and baking soda into the mixture and stir in carefully. Stir in the chocolate chips and walnuts. Drop dessertspoonfuls of the mixture onto the prepared cookie sheets, spaced well apart to allow for spreading.

• Bake in the oven for 10–15 minutes, or until the mixture has spread and the cookies are beginning to feel firm. Remove from the oven and let cool on the cookie sheets for 2 minutes, before transfering to cooling racks.

MAKES 24

¾ cup unsalted butter or margarine,
   plus extra for greasing
1 cup soft brown sugar
1 egg
½ cup all-purpose flour
1 tsp baking soda
pinch of salt

scant ½ cup whole-wheat flour
1 tbsp bran
1⅓ cups semisweet chocolate chips
generous 2 cups rolled oats
1 tbsp strong coffee
⅔ cup hazelnuts, toasted and
   chopped coarsely

Chocolate and Coffee Whole-Wheat Cookies

These delicious dark cookies, flavored with coffee and toasted chopped hazelnuts, are perfect served with coffee.

• Preheat the oven to 375°F/190°C. Grease 2 large cookie sheets. Cream the butter and sugar together in a bowl. Add the egg and beat well, using a hand whisk if preferred.

• In a separate bowl, sift together the all-purpose flour, baking soda, and salt, then add in the whole-wheat flour and bran. Mix in the egg mixture, then stir in the chocolate chips, oats, coffee, and hazelnuts. Mix well, with an electric whisk if preferred.

• Put 24 rounded tablespoonfuls of the mixture onto the prepared cookie sheets, leaving room for the cookies to spread during cooking. Alternatively, with lightly floured hands, break off pieces of the mixture and roll into balls (about 1 oz/25 g each), then place on the cookie sheets and flatten them with the back of a teaspoon. Transfer the cookie sheets to the preheated oven and bake for 16–18 minutes, or until the cookies are golden brown.

• Remove from the oven, then transfer to a cooling rack and let cool before serving.

MAKES 18–20

2 squares bittersweet chocolate, broken into pieces

1 cup all-purpose flour

1 tsp baking powder

1 egg

scant ¾ cup superfine sugar

½ tsp vanilla extract

scant ¼ cup corn oil, plus extra for oiling

2 tbsp confectioners' sugar

1 small package milk chocolate buttons (about 30 buttons)

1 small package white chocolate buttons (about 30 buttons)

Zebra Cookies

If chocolate buttons are difficult to find, substitute 1 small package with ⅓ cup chocolate chips.

• Melt the bittersweet chocolate in a heatproof bowl set over a pan of gently simmering water. Remove from the heat and let cool. Sift the flour and baking powder together.

• Meanwhile, in a large bowl, whisk the egg, sugar, oil, and vanilla extract together. Whisk in the cooled, melted chocolate until well blended, then gradually stir in the flour. Cover the bowl with plastic wrap and chill in the refrigerator for at least 3 hours.

• Preheat the oven to 375°F/190°C. Oil 1–2 large cookie sheets. Shape tablespoonfuls of the mixture into log shapes using your hands, each measuring about 2 inches/5 cm. Roll the logs generously in the confectioners' sugar, then place on the prepared cookie sheets, allowing room for the cookies to spread during cooking.

• Bake the cookies in the preheated oven for 15 minutes, or until firm. Remove from the oven, and place 3 chocolate buttons down the center of each, alternating the colors. Transfer to a cooling rack and let cool.

MAKES 20

1 stick unsalted butter, softened,
    plus extra for greasing

generous ½ cup light
    muscovado sugar

1 egg

⅔ cup oatmeal

1 tbsp milk

1 tsp vanilla extract

scant 1 cup all-purpose flour

1 tbsp unsweetened cocoa

½ tsp baking powder

6 squares bittersweet chocolate,
    broken into pieces

6 squares milk chocolate,
    broken into pieces

Chocolate Chip Oaties

After baking, cookies must be left on the cookie sheet for 2 minutes, because this ensures they do not fall apart when transferred to a cooling rack.

• Preheat the oven to 350°F/180°C. Grease 2 large cookie sheets. Place the butter and sugar in a bowl and beat together with a wooden spoon until light and fluffy.

• Beat in the egg, then add the oatmeal, milk, and vanilla. Beat together until well blended. Sift the flour, cocoa, and baking powder into the mixture and stir. Stir in the chocolate pieces.

• Place dessertspoonfuls of the mixture on the prepared cookie sheets and flatten slightly with a fork. Bake in the preheated oven for 15 minutes, or until slightly risen and firm. Remove from the oven and cool on the cookie sheets for 2 minutes, then transfer to cooling racks to cool completely.

MAKES 24

generous ¾ cup unsalted butter,
  plus extra for greasing

12½ squares bittersweet chocolate

1 tsp strong coffee

2 eggs

scant ¾ cup soft brown sugar

scant 1¼ cups all-purpose flour

¼ tsp baking powder

pinch of salt

2 tsp almond extract

generous ½ cup Brazil nuts, chopped

generous ½ cup hazelnuts, chopped

1½ squares white chocolate

Chocolate Temptations

Piping white and dark chocolate lines over these cookies gives them a touch of elegance and sophistication.

• Preheat the oven to 350°F/180°C. Grease 1–2 large cookie sheets. Put 8 squares of the bittersweet chocolate with the butter and coffee into a heatproof bowl set over a pan of gently simmering water and heat until the chocolate is almost melted.

• Meanwhile, beat the eggs in a bowl until fluffy. Gradually whisk in the sugar until thick. Remove the chocolate from the heat and stir until smooth. Add to the egg mixture and stir until combined.

• Sift the flour, baking powder, and salt into a bowl, then stir into the chocolate mixture. Chop 3 squares of the remaining bittersweet chocolate into pieces and stir into the mixture. Stir in the almond extract and chopped nuts.

• Put 24 tablespoonfuls of the mixture onto the cookie sheet, then transfer to the preheated oven and bake for 16 minutes. Remove from the oven and transfer to a cooling rack to cool. To decorate, melt the remaining chocolate (plain and white) in turn as earlier, then spoon into a pastry bag and pipe thin lines onto the cookies.

MAKES 9

scant 6 tbsp unsalted butter or
    margarine, plus extra for greasing
8 oz/225 g chocolate graham crackers
7 fl oz/200 ml canned evaporated milk
1 egg, beaten
1 tsp vanilla extract

2 tbsp superfine sugar
scant ⅓ cup self-rising flour, sifted
scant 1⅓ cups dry unsweetened
    coconut
1¾ squares semisweet chocolate
    (optional)

Chocolate Coconut Layers

You can store the squares in an airtight container for up to 4 days. They can be frozen, undecorated, for up to 2 months. Defrost at room temperature.

• Preheat the oven to 375°F/190°C. Grease a shallow 8-inch/20-cm square cake pan and line the bottom with parchment paper.
• Crush the crackers in a plastic bag with a rolling pin or process them in a food processor. Melt the butter in a pan and stir in the crushed crackers thoroughly. Remove from the heat and press the mixture into the bottom of the prepared cake pan.
• In a separate bowl, beat together the evaporated milk, egg, vanilla, and sugar until smooth. Stir in the flour and grated coconut. Pour over the cracker layer and use a spatula to smooth the top.
• Bake in the preheated oven for 30 minutes, or until the coconut topping has become firm and just golden. Remove from the oven and let cool in the cake pan for about 5 minutes, then cut into squares. Let cool completely in the pan.
• Carefully remove the squares from the pan and place them on a cutting board. Melt the semisweet chocolate (if using) and drizzle it over the squares to decorate them. Let the chocolate set before serving.

MAKES 9

1 stick unsalted butter,
   plus extra for greasing

8 squares white chocolate

¾ cup walnut pieces

2 eggs

generous ½ cup soft brown sugar

generous ⅔ cup self-rising flour

White Chocolate Brownies

You can vary the nuts in this recipe by using almonds, pecans, or hazelnuts instead of the walnuts.

• Preheat the oven to 350°F/180°C. Lightly grease a 7-inch/18-cm square cake pan.

• Coarsely chop 6 squares of white chocolate and all the walnuts. Put the remaining chocolate and the butter in a heatproof bowl set over a pan of gently simmering water. When melted, stir together, then set aside to cool slightly.

• Whisk the eggs and sugar together, then beat in the cooled chocolate mixture until well mixed. Fold in the flour, chopped chocolate, and the walnuts. Turn the mixture into the prepared pan and smooth the surface.

• Transfer the pan to the preheated oven and bake for 30 minutes, or until just set. The mixture should still be a little soft in the center. Remove from the oven and let cool in the pan, then cut into 9 squares before serving.

MAKES 20

6 tbsp unsalted butter, plus extra
    for greasing
½ cup raw brown sugar
1 egg
scant ¼ cup wheatgerm

generous ¾ cup whole-wheat
    self-rising flour
6 tbsp self-rising flour, sifted
4½ squares semisweet chocolate,
    broken into pieces

Chocolate Wheatmeals

These cookies can be frozen very successfully. Freeze them after they have cooled completely but before dipping in the melted chocolate. Thaw, then dip them in melted chocolate and let set before serving.

• Preheat the oven to 350°F/180°C. Grease 1–2 cookie sheets. Beat the butter and sugar together in a bowl until fluffy. Add the egg and beat well. Stir in the wheatgerm and flours. Bring the mixture together with your hands.

• Roll rounded teaspoons of the mixture into balls and place on the prepared cookie sheet or sheets, spaced well apart to allow for spreading. Flatten the cookies slightly with a fork, then bake in the preheated oven for 15–20 minutes, or until golden.

• Remove from the oven and let cool on the cookie sheets for a few minutes before transferring to a cooling rack to cool completely.

• Melt the chocolate in a heatproof bowl set over a pan of gently simmering water, then dip each cookie in the chocolate to cover the base and a little way up the sides. Let the excess chocolate drip back into the bowl. Place the cookies on a sheet of parchment paper and let set in a cool place before serving.

SERVES 16

4 tbsp unsalted butter, plus extra
    for greasing
¼ cup superfine sugar
generous ⅔ cup all-purpose flour

1¼ cups confectioners' sugar
1–2 tbsp warm water
½ tsp peppermint extract
6 squares bittersweet chocolate,
    broken into pieces

Chocolate Peppermint Slices

Be careful when measuring the peppermint extract and do not hold the spoon directly over the bowl. If you accidentally add more than you intend and it splashes into the confectioners' sugar mixture, you may find the topping too hot to handle.

• Preheat the oven to 350°F/180°C. Grease an 8 x 12-inch/20 x 30-cm jelly roll pan and line with parchment paper. Beat the butter and sugar together until pale and fluffy. Stir in the flour until the mixture binds together.

• Knead the mixture to form a smooth dough, then press into the prepared pan. Prick the surface all over with a fork. Bake in the preheated oven for 10–15 minutes, or until lightly browned and just firm to the touch. Remove from the oven and let cool in the pan.

• Sift the confectioners' sugar into a bowl. Gradually add the water, then add the peppermint extract. Spread the frosting over the base, then let set.

• Melt the chocolate in a heatproof bowl set over a pan of gently simmering water, then remove from the heat and spread over the frosting. Let set, then cut into slices.

MAKES 12

1 stick unsalted butter, plus extra
    for greasing
scant 1¼ cups all-purpose flour
¼ cup golden superfine sugar

FILLING AND TOPPING

1¾ sticks butter
generous ½ cup golden
    superfine sugar
3 tbsp corn syrup
14 fl oz/400 ml canned
    condensed milk
7 squares bittersweet chocolate,
    broken into pieces

Caramel Chocolate Shortbread

Take great care when cooking the caramel filling because it can very easily catch and burn on the bottom of the pan. Stir the mixture constantly until it has thickened.

• Preheat the oven to 350°F/180°C. Grease a 9-inch/23-cm shallow square cake pan and line the bottom with parchment paper. Place the butter, flour, and sugar in a food processor and process until they begin to bind together. Press the mixture into the prepared pan and smooth the top. Bake in the preheated oven for 20–25 minutes, or until golden.

• Meanwhile, make the filling. Place the butter, sugar, syrup, and condensed milk in a pan and heat gently until the sugar has dissolved. Bring to a boil and simmer for 6–8 minutes, stirring constantly, until the mixture becomes very thick. Remove the shortbread from the oven, then pour over the filling and chill in the refrigerator until firm.

• To make the topping, melt the chocolate in a heatproof bowl set over a pan of gently simmering water. Remove from the heat and let cool slightly, then spread over the caramel. Chill in the refrigerator until set. Cut it into 12 pieces with a sharp knife and serve.

Nuts are positive powerhouses of energy, so when you need a pick-me-up, whether with a well-earned morning mug of coffee or a restorative cup of tea in the afternoon, this chapter is packed with just what the doctor ordered. The cookies and bars in this chapter are great for lunch boxes for the children, too—especially because with homemade cookies, *you* choose just how much sugar and salt you want to include. A pecan cookie or a bar of hazelnut crunch, served with a glass of milk or fruit juice, will also satisfy after-school hunger pangs. In this chapter almonds, hazelnuts, pecans, and walnuts are matched with tasty combinations of oats, spices, chocolate, syrup, fruit, and even coffee to produce delectable nibbles for any time of day when you fancy a nourishing snack. And what could be nicer than homemade cookies served with dessert at the end of a dinner party?

NUTTY BUT NICE

Nuts have a short storage life and can turn rancid very rapidly, so it is best to buy them in small quantities, as and when you need them, and store them in airtight containers in a cool, dark place. In any case, keep an eye on the "use by" date on the packaging. For best results, buy nuts in their shells and crack them open when you want to use them. Although this is time-consuming, the flavor and texture will be much better than using ready-shelled nuts. Discard any nuts with signs of mold on the shells or kernels, for not only will these taste absolutely horrible, spoiling all your hard work in mixing the cookie dough, they may contain toxins, which can cause unpleasant or even serious illness.

MAKES 9

1 stick unsalted butter, plus extra
    for greasing
scant 1¼ cups soft brown sugar
1 egg

1 egg yolk
1 cup self-rising flour
1 tsp ground cinnamon
¾ cup walnuts, coarsely chopped

Walnut and Cinnamon Blondies

Do not chop the walnuts too finely, because the blondies should have a good texture and a slight crunch to them.

• Preheat the oven to 350°F/180°C. Grease the base and sides of a 7-inch/18-cm square cake pan and line with parchment paper. Place the butter and sugar in a pan over low heat and stir until the sugar has dissolved. Cook, stirring, for 1 minute more. The mixture will bubble slightly, but do not let it boil. Let cool for 10 minutes.

• Stir the egg and egg yolk into the mixture. Sift in the flour and cinnamon, then add the nuts and stir until just blended. Pour the cake mixture into the prepared pan and bake in the preheated oven for 20–25 minutes, or until springy in the middle and a toothpick inserted into the center comes out clean.

• Let cool in the pan for a few minutes, then run a knife around the edge of the pan to loosen. Turn out onto a cooling rack and peel off the paper. Let cool completely. When cold, cut into squares.

MAKES 15

1 stick unsalted butter, softened, plus
    extra for greasing
scant ½ cup light muscovado sugar
1 egg, beaten

⅓ cup pecans, chopped
generous ½ cup all-purpose flour
½ tsp baking powder
⅓ cup oatmeal

Oatie Pecan Cookies

To save a lot of hard work, beat the butter and sugar together with an electric hand-held mixer. Alternatively, use a food processor.

• Preheat the oven to 350°F/180°C, then grease 2 cookie sheets. Place the butter and sugar in a bowl and beat until light and fluffy. Gradually beat in the egg, then stir in the nuts.

• Sift the flour and baking powder into the mixture and add the oats. Stir together until well combined. Drop dessertspoonfuls of the mixture onto the prepared cookie sheets, spaced well apart to allow for spreading.

• Bake in the preheated oven for 15 minutes, or until pale golden. Remove from the oven and let cool on the cookie sheets for 2 minutes, then transfer to cooling racks to cool completely.

MAKES 8
3 eggs
2/3 cup ground almonds
scant 1½ cups milk powder

1 cup granulated sugar
½ tsp saffron threads
1 stick unsalted butter
1 tbsp slivered almonds, to decorate

Almond Slices

These almond slices are best eaten hot, but they may also be served cold. They can be made a day or even a week in advance and reheated. They also freeze beautifully.

• Preheat the oven to 325°F/160°C. Lightly beat the eggs together in a mixing bowl and set aside.
• Place the ground almonds, milk powder, sugar, and saffron in a large mixing bowl and stir to mix well.
• Melt the butter in a small pan over low heat. Pour the melted butter over the dry ingredients and mix well with a wooden spoon until thoroughly combined.
• Add the beaten eggs to the mixture in the pan and stir to blend well.
• Spread the mixture evenly in a shallow 8-inch/20-cm ovenproof dish and bake in the preheated oven for 45 minutes, or until a toothpick inserted into the center comes out clean.
• Remove from the oven and cut into slices. Decorate the slices with slivered almonds and transfer to serving plates. Serve hot or cold.

MAKES 30

¾ cup unsalted butter or margarine,
    plus extra for greasing
scant 1¼ cups raw brown sugar
1 egg, beaten
4 tbsp milk
1 tsp vanilla extract
½ tsp almond extract

generous ⅔ cup hazelnuts
1 cup all-purpose flour
1½ tsp ground allspice
¼ tsp baking soda
pinch of salt
2 cups oatmeal
scant 1 cup golden raisins

Oat and Hazelnut Morsels

Try these delicious cookies with a refreshing cup of mint tea in the afternoon, or give them to hungry children as a healthy snack.

• Preheat the oven to 375°F/190°C. Grease 2 large cookie sheets.
• Cream the butter and sugar together in a mixing bowl. Blend in the egg, milk, and vanilla and almond extracts until thoroughly combined. Chop the hazelnuts finely.
• In a mixing bowl, sift the flour, allspice, baking soda, and salt together. Add to the creamed mixture slowly, stirring constantly. Mix in the oatmeal, golden raisins, and hazelnuts.
• Put 30 rounded tablespoonfuls of the mixture onto the prepared cookie sheets, spaced well apart to allow for spreading. Transfer to the preheated oven and bake for 12–15 minutes, or until the cookies are golden brown.
• Remove the cookies from the oven and place on a cooling rack to cool before serving.

MAKES 20

2 sticks unsalted butter, plus extra
    for greasing
2½ squares bittersweet chocolate
scant 1 cup all-purpose flour
¾ tsp baking soda

¼ tsp baking powder
⅓ cup pecans
½ cup raw brown sugar
½ tsp almond extract
1 egg
1 tsp milk

Pecan Brownies

Pecans are very similar to walnuts, which you can substitute if you prefer.

• Preheat the oven to 350°F/180°C. Grease a large baking dish and line it with parchment paper.
• Put the chocolate in a heatproof bowl set over a pan of gently simmering water and heat until it is melted. Meanwhile, sift together the flour, baking soda, and baking powder into a large bowl.
• Finely chop the pecans and set aside. In a separate bowl, cream together the butter and sugar, then mix in the almond extract and the egg. Remove the chocolate from the heat and stir into the butter mixture. Add the flour mixture, milk, and chopped nuts to the bowl and stir until well combined.
• Spoon the mixture into the prepared baking dish and smooth it. Transfer to the preheated oven and cook for 30 minutes, or until firm to the touch (it should still be a little soft in the center). Remove from the oven and let cool completely. Cut into 20 squares and serve.

MAKES ABOUT 60
1⅜ sticks unsalted butter, at room
    temperature, plus extra for
    greasing
¾ cup superfine sugar
generous ¾ cup all-purpose flour

generous ¼ cup ground almonds
pinch of salt
½ cup blanched almonds, lightly
    toasted and finely chopped
finely grated rind of 1 large lemon
4 egg whites

Almond Cookies

You can toast almonds by dry-frying them in a heavy-bottom skillet or by spreading them out on a cookie sheet and placing in a preheated oven, 350°F/180°C. They take only a few minutes and it's important to watch them carefully because they burn easily.

• Preheat the oven to 350°F/180°C. Grease 2 cookie sheets. Put the butter and sugar into a bowl and beat until light and fluffy. Sift over the flour, ground almonds, and salt, tipping in any ground almonds left in the strainer. Use a large metal spoon to fold in the chopped almonds and grated lemon rind.
• In a separate, grease-free bowl, whisk the egg whites until soft peaks form. Fold these into the almond mixture.
• Drop small teaspoonfuls of the cookie mixture onto the prepared cookie sheets, spacing them very well apart to allow for spreading. (You might need to cook in batches.) Bake in a preheated oven for 15–20 minutes, or until golden brown around the edges. Remove from the oven and transfer to a cooling rack to cool completely. Continue baking until all the mixture is used. Store the cookies in an airtight container for up to 1 week.

MAKES 18

2 sticks unsalted butter,
  plus extra for greasing

1 cup walnut pieces

⅞ cup superfine sugar

few drops vanilla extract

1½ cups all-purpose flour

scant 1¼ cups bittersweet
  chocolate chips

Walnut and Chocolate Chip Slices

Unsalted butter is always better when you are baking sweet treats. It's also ideal for greasing because it is less likely to burn than salted butter. As an alternative, you could brush the cookie sheet with a bland oil, such as corn.

• Preheat the oven to 350°F/180°C. Grease an 8 x 12-inch/20 x 30-cm jelly roll pan. Coarsely chop the walnut pieces to about the same size as the chocolate chips.

• Beat the butter and sugar together until pale and fluffy. Add the vanilla extract, then stir in the flour. Stir in the walnuts and chocolate chips. Press the mixture into the prepared pan. Bake the mixture in the preheated oven for 20–25 minutes, or until golden brown. Remove from the oven. Cool in the pan and cut into slices.

MAKES ABOUT 16

1 stick unsalted butter, softened, plus
  extra for greasing
generous ½ cup light muscovado
  sugar
scant ½ cup golden granulated sugar
1 tsp vanilla extract
1 tbsp instant coffee granules,
  dissolved in 1 tbsp hot water

1 egg
scant 1¼ cups all-purpose flour
½ tsp baking powder
¼ tsp baking soda
⅓ cup milk chocolate chips
½ cup shelled walnuts, coarsely
  chopped

Mocha Walnut Cookies

Muscovado sugar has a tendency to be quite lumpy, so it is a good idea to sift it before use when baking cakes and cookies.

• Preheat the oven to 350°F/180°C. Grease 2 large cookie sheets with a little butter. Place the butter, muscovado sugar, and granulated sugar in a large bowl and beat together thoroughly until light and fluffy. Place the vanilla extract, coffee, and egg in a separate large bowl and whisk together.

• Gradually add the coffee mixture to the butter and sugar, beating until fluffy. Sift the flour, baking powder, and baking soda into the mixture and fold in carefully. Fold in the chocolate chips and walnuts.

• Drop dessertspoonfuls of the mixture onto the prepared cookie sheets, spacing well apart to allow room for spreading. Bake in the preheated oven for 10–15 minutes, or until crisp on the outside but still soft inside. Remove from the oven. Cool on the cookie sheets for 2 minutes, then transfer to cooling racks to cool completely.

MAKES 12
1 stick unsalted butter, plus extra
　for greasing
generous 2 cups rolled oats
⅓ cup hazelnuts, lightly toasted
　and chopped

generous ⅓ cup all-purpose flour
scant ½ cup light muscovado sugar
2 tbsp corn syrup
⅓ cup bittersweet chocolate chips

Hazelnut Chocolate Crunch

Instead of using a pan, heat the butter, sugar, and syrup in a microwave oven on Medium for 2½ minutes.

• Preheat the oven to 350°F/180°C. Grease a 9-inch/23-cm shallow, square baking pan. Mix the oats, nuts, and flour in a large bowl.

• Place the butter, sugar, and syrup in a large pan and heat gently until the sugar has dissolved. Pour in the dry ingredients and mix well. Stir in the chocolate chips.

• Turn the mixture into the prepared pan and bake in the preheated oven for 20–25 minutes, or until golden brown and firm to the touch. Using a knife, mark into 12 rectangles and let cool in the pan. Cut the hazelnut chocolate crunch bars with a sharp knife before carefully removing them from the pan.

MAKES 24

1¾ sticks unsalted butter, plus
   extra for greasing
1⅜ cups raw brown sugar
1 egg
scant 1 cup all-purpose flour, sifted
1 tsp baking powder

1 tsp baking soda
scant 1 cup oatmeal
1 tbsp bran
1 tbsp wheatgerm
4 oz/115 g mixed nuts, toasted
   and coarsely chopped

generous 1 cup bittersweet
   chocolate chips
generous ¾ cup raisins and
   golden raisins
6 squares semisweet chocolate,
   coarsely chopped

Nutty Drizzles

Do not replace oatmeal
with rolled oats, which
have been rolled into
thin flakes.

• Preheat the oven to 350°F/180°C. Grease 2 large cookie sheets. In a large bowl, cream together the butter, sugar, and egg. Add the flour, baking powder, baking soda, oatmeal, bran, and wheatgerm and mix together until well combined. Finally, stir in the nuts, chocolate chips, and dried fruit.

• Put 24 rounded tablespoonfuls of the mixture onto the prepared cookie sheets. Transfer to the preheated oven and bake for 12 minutes, or until the cookies are golden brown.

• Remove the cookies from the oven, then transfer to a cooling rack and let cool. Meanwhile, heat the chocolate pieces in a heatproof bowl set over a pan of gently simmering water until melted. Stir the chocolate, then let cool slightly. Use a spoon to drizzle the chocolate in waves over the cookies, or spoon it into a pastry bag and pipe zigzag lines over the cookies. When the chocolate has set, store the cookies in an airtight container in the refrigerator until ready to serve.

Nutritionists recommend that we eat five portions of fruit and vegetables a day, but this is not always practical and can prove to be quite a problem if you have fussy eaters in your household. The scrumptious nibbles in this chapter include apricots, figs, cherries, dates, currants, raisins, golden raisins, and bananas, combined with a mouthwatering range of other ingredients as varied as nuts, seeds, oats, honey, spices, chocolate, and fruit juice. They are sure to be a runaway success with every member of the family—and, of course, there is no need for you to tell anyone that these tasty snacks are actually quite healthy too.

Fruit bars are ideal for the school lunch box and can also provide a kick-start to the day for busy adults who have no time for breakfast. They make a great pick-me-up whenever your energy is flagging and are the perfect after-school snack for kids.

FRUITFUL ENDEAVORS

From Apricot Oat-Style Cookies to Caribbean Cookies, the recipes in this chapter are easy to follow, quick, and economical, so there is no excuse for not having a ready supply of tasty treats to hand. Furthermore, many of the ingredients for these cookies and bars are pantry staples, such as honey, oatmeal, and dried fruit. It is easy to substitute one kind of dried fruit for another—dates instead of figs or golden raisins instead of raisins—so you can customize your baking to your resources and, more importantly, to your family's tastes. Keep an eye on the "use-by" dates on the packages to ensure that your cookies have the freshest flavor.

MAKES 10

corn oil, for oiling

¾ cup polyunsaturated spread

scant ½ cup raw brown sugar

clear honey

generous ¾ cup no-soak dried
apricots, chopped

2 tsp sesame seeds

1½ cups oatmeal

Apricot Oat-Style Cookies

No-soak dried apricots
are ideal for this recipe
because soaking takes
around 30 minutes. You
could also use dried figs,
dates, or muscatel raisins
for a change of flavor.

• Preheat the oven to 350°F/180°C. Very lightly oil a 10½ x 6½-inch/26 x 17-cm shallow cake pan.
• Put the spread, sugar, and honey into a small pan over low heat and heat until the ingredients have melted together—do not let the mixture boil. When the ingredients are warm and well combined, stir in the apricots, sesame seeds, and oats.
• Spoon the mixture into the prepared pan and lightly level with the back of a spoon. Cook in the preheated oven for 20–25 minutes, or until golden brown. Remove from the oven, then cut into 10 bars and let cool completely before removing from the cake pan. Store the flapjacks in an airtight container and consume within 2–3 days.

MAKES 20

1 cup unsalted butter or margarine,
   plus extra for greasing

scant ½ cup dried figs

⅓ cup clear honey

4 tbsp raw brown sugar

2 eggs, beaten

pinch of salt

1 tsp allspice

1 tsp baking soda

½ tsp vanilla extract

2 tbsp dried dates, finely chopped

1½ cups all-purpose flour

2 cups oatmeal

⅜ cup walnuts, finely chopped

dried fig pieces, to decorate (optional)

Fig and Walnut Cookies

When making cream mixtures, remove the butter from the refrigerator about 30 minutes before you need to use it to let it come to room temperature and soften slightly.

• Preheat the oven to 350°F/180°C. Grease 2 large cookie sheets.

• Finely chop the figs. Mix the butter, honey, figs, and sugar together in a large bowl. Beat the eggs into the mixture and mix thoroughly.

• In a separate bowl, combine the salt, allspice, baking soda, vanilla extract, and dates. Gradually stir them into the creamed mixture. Sift the flour into the mixture and stir well. Finally, mix in the oatmeal and walnuts.

• Drop 20 rounded tablespoonfuls of the mixture onto the prepared cookie sheets, spaced well apart to allow for spreading. Decorate with fig pieces, if using. Bake in the preheated oven for 10–15 minutes, or until the cookies are golden brown.

• Remove the cookies from the oven. Transfer to a cooling rack and let cool before serving.

MAKES ABOUT 14

4 tbsp unsalted butter

scant ¼ cup raw brown sugar

1 tbsp corn syrup

generous ⅓ cup all-purpose flour,
    sifted

⅛ cup angelica, coarsely chopped

⅛ cup candied cherries, coarsely
    chopped

½ cup slivered almonds,
    coarsely chopped

⅓ cup candied pineapple,
    coarsely chopped

1 tsp lemon juice

4 squares bittersweet chocolate,
    melted and cooled

Pineapple and Cherry Florentines

If you have difficulty removing the florentines from the cookie sheet, return them to the oven for 2 minutes, then lift off and cool on a cooling rack.

• Preheat the oven to 350°F/180°C. Line 1 or 2 large cookie sheets with nonstick parchment paper. Place the butter, sugar, and syrup in a pan and heat gently until melted, then stir in the flour, angelica, cherries, almonds, pineapple, and lemon juice.

• Place walnut-size mounds of the mixture spaced well apart on the prepared baking sheets and flatten gently with a fork. Bake in the preheated oven for 8–10 minutes, or until golden brown. Use a spatula to neaten the ragged edges. Let cool for 1 minute, then transfer to a cooling rack to cool completely.

• Spread the melted chocolate over the base of each florentine, then place chocolate-side up on a cooling rack. Use a fork to mark the chocolate with wavy lines. Let stand until set.

MAKES 36

generous ½ cup unsalted butter or
    margarine, plus extra for greasing
1 cup no-soak dried apricots
½ cup dried dates
1 cup all-purpose flour
½ cup oatmeal

generous 1 cup wheat flakes
½ tsp baking soda
pinch of salt
scant ¼ cup soft brown sugar,
    plus extra for dusting
2 eggs
1 tsp almond extract

Fruit Morsels

You can chop dried fruit with a heavy-bladed kitchen knife or snip it into pieces with a pair of strong kitchen scissors— whichever is easier.

• Preheat the oven to 375°F/190°C. Grease 2 large cookie sheets with butter. Chop the dried apricots and dates. Sift the flour into a large bowl and mix in the oatmeal, wheat flakes, baking soda, and salt.

• In a separate bowl, blend together the sugar and butter. Beat in the eggs until the mixture is light and fluffy. Gradually add the flour mixture, stirring. Blend in the almond extract and fruit. Mix well.

• Drop 36 teaspoonfuls of the mixture onto the prepared cookie sheets, spaced very well apart to allow for spreading. Dust with sugar. Bake for 10 minutes, or until golden brown.

• Remove the cookies from the oven. Place on a cooling rack and let cool before serving.

MAKES 24

1½ sticks unsalted butter, softened,
  plus extra for greasing

scant 1 cup golden superfine sugar

1 egg, beaten

2 tbsp milk

⅓ cup chopped candied peel

generous ⅔ cup currants

2⅓ cups all-purpose flour,
  plus extra for dusting

1 tsp allspice

GLAZE

1 egg white, lightly beaten

2 tbsp golden superfine sugar

Easter Cookies

Be careful when sprinkling the sugar over the glaze—any sugar sprinkled directly onto the cookie sheet will burn onto its surface.

• Preheat the oven to 350°F/180°C, then grease 2 large cookie sheets. Place the butter and sugar in a bowl and beat until light and fluffy. Gradually beat in the egg and milk. Stir in the mixed peel and currants, then sift in the flour and allspice. Mix together to make a firm dough. Knead lightly until smooth.

• On a floured counter, roll out the dough to ¼ inch/5 mm thick and use a 2-inch/5-cm round cookie cutter to stamp out the cookies. Re-roll the dough trimmings and stamp out more cookies until the dough is used up. Place the cookies on the prepared cookie sheets and bake in the preheated oven for 10 minutes.

• Remove from the oven to glaze. Brush with the egg white and sprinkle with the superfine sugar, then return to the oven for an additional 5 minutes, or until lightly browned. Let cool on the cookie sheets for 2 minutes, then transfer to cooling racks to cool completely.

MAKES 24
unsalted butter, for greasing
1 oz/25 g mashed banana
1 tbsp pineapple juice
1 tbsp orange juice
4 tbsp peanut oil
1 egg

1 tbsp milk
1 cup all-purpose flour
¼ tsp baking soda
scant 1 cup dry unsweetened
    coconut
raw brown sugar, for sprinkling

Caribbean Cookies

If you prefer, you could substitute grated fresh coconut for the dry unsweetened kind. You could also use finely chopped, very ripe mango instead of the banana.

• Preheat the oven to 350°F/180°C. Grease a large cookie sheet.
• In a large bowl, cream together the banana, fruit juices, oil, egg, and milk. Transfer the mixture to a food mixer. With the machine running, sift in the flour and baking soda, beating constantly. Add the dry unsweetened coconut and mix well.
• Drop rounded teaspoonfuls onto the prepared cookie sheet, spaced well apart to allow for spreading. Sprinkle with the raw brown sugar, then transfer to the preheated oven and bake for about 10 minutes, or until the cookies are golden brown.
• Remove the cookies from the oven and transfer to a cooling rack to cool before serving.

MAKES 9 SQUARES

1 stick unsalted butter, plus extra
for greasing

2 tbsp clear honey

1 egg, beaten

scant 1 cup ground almonds

2/3 cup no-soak dried apricots,
finely chopped

1/3 cup dried cherries

1/3 cup toasted hazelnuts

2 tbsp sesame seeds

1 cup jumbo oats

Fruit and Nut Squares

The easiest way to smooth the surface of the mixture is with the back of a slightly damp tablespoon or a damp spatula. Smoothing the surface ensures that the mixture bakes through and is an even golden brown.

• Preheat the oven to 350°F/180°C. Lightly grease a 7-inch/18-cm shallow, square cake pan with butter. Beat the remaining butter with the honey in a bowl until creamy, then beat in the egg with the almonds.

• Add the remaining ingredients and mix together well. Press into the pan, ensuring that the mixture is firmly packed. Smooth the top.

• Transfer to the preheated oven and bake for 20–25 minutes, or until firm to the touch and golden brown.

• Remove from the oven and let stand for 10 minutes before marking into squares. Let stand until cold before removing from the pan. Cut into squares and store in an airtight container and consume within 2–3 days.

MAKES 30

¾ cup unsalted butter or margarine,
   plus extra for greasing

1 cup soft brown sugar

2 eggs

2⅓ cups all-purpose flour

pinch of salt

2 tsp baking powder

2 tbsp milk

1 tsp almond extract

scant 1½ cups chopped walnuts

scant ½ cup raisins

scant ½ cup golden raisins

½ cup maraschino cherries

7 oz/200 g wheat flakes, crushed

15 maraschino cherries, halved,
   to decorate

Cherry and Walnut Cookies

The slightly bitter flavor of maraschino cherries gives these cookies an intriguing flavor. However, you could use sweet cherries if you prefer.

• Preheat the oven to 375°F/190°C. Grease 1 or 2 large cookie sheets.

• Cream the butter and sugar in a large mixing bowl until the mixture is light and fluffy. Beat the eggs into the butter and sugar mixture.

• Gradually sift the flour, salt, and baking powder into the creamed mixture. Add the milk and almond extract and mix thoroughly. Stir the walnuts, dried fruit, and maraschino cherries into the mixture.

• Form the dough into 30 balls (about 1 rounded tablespoon each) and roll in the crushed wheat flakes. Place the dough balls on the prepared cookie sheet, spaced about 1 inch/2.5 cm apart. Place half a maraschino cherry on the top of each dough ball. Transfer to the preheated oven and cook for 10 minutes, or until the cookies are light brown. Transfer from the oven to a cooling rack and let cool completely before serving.

MAKES 16

1¾ sticks unsalted butter,
    plus extra for greasing
1 cup raw brown sugar
2 tbsp corn syrup

scant 2 cups oatmeal
generous 1 cup dry unsweetened
    coconut
generous ⅓ cup candied cherries,
    chopped

Coconut Oat-Style Cookies

The cookies are best stored in an airtight container and eaten within 1 week. They can also be frozen for up to 1 month.

• Preheat the oven to 325°F/160°C. Grease a 12 x 9-inch/30 x 23-cm baking sheet.
• Put the butter, sugar, and syrup in a large pan and set over low heat until just melted. Stir in the oats, coconut, and cherries and mix until evenly combined.
• Spread the mixture evenly onto the baking tray and press down with a spatula to make a smooth surface.
• Bake in the preheated oven for 30 minutes. Remove from the oven and let cool on the baking sheet for 10 minutes. Using a sharp knife, cut the cookies into rectangles. Carefully transfer the pieces to a cooling rack and let cool completely.

MAKES 16

1½ cups all-purpose flour

1 tsp baking powder

½ cup superfine sugar

scant ½ cup soft brown sugar

2 sticks unsalted butter

1 cup oatmeal

2/3 cup strawberry jelly

scant 2/3 cup semisweet
chocolate chips

scant ¼ cup almonds,
chopped

Strawberry and Chocolate Slices

Other flavors of jelly also go well with chocolate. Raspberry is a classic partner, but you may want to strain out any seeds before spreading it over the cooked base.

• Preheat the oven to 375°F/190°C. Line a 12 x 8-inch/30 x 20-cm deep-sided jelly roll pan with parchment paper. Sift the flour and baking powder into a large bowl.

• Add the superfine sugar and brown sugar to the flour and mix well. Add the butter and rub in until the mixture resembles bread crumbs. Stir in the oatmeal.

• Press three-quarters of the mixture into the bottom of the prepared cake pan. Bake in the preheated oven for 10 minutes.

• Spread the jelly over the cooked base, then sprinkle over the chocolate chips. Mix the remaining flour mixture with the almonds. Sprinkle evenly over the chocolate chips and press down gently.

• Return to the oven and bake for an additional 20–25 minutes, or until golden brown. Remove from the oven and let cool in the pan, then cut into slices.

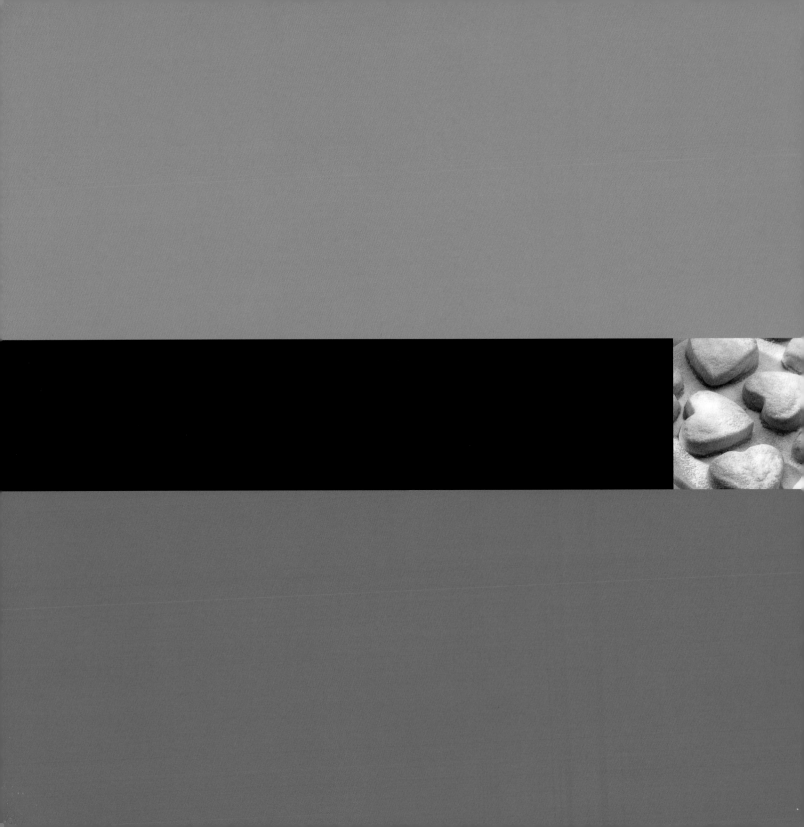

All homemade cookies and bars are special, but the ones in this chapter have that little something extra, whether charming, dainty Vanilla Hearts—perfect for a wedding anniversary morning tea tray—or Lavender Cookies—the epitome of an elegant tea party on the lawn.

Lots of occasions call for a special treat, and in this chapter you are sure to find a delicious but easy recipe for just the right tempting little snack, whether for a fund-raising coffee morning, a tea tray to welcome new neighbors, a school summer fair, or just to spoil the family. Homemade cookies also make delightful gifts, especially if you pack them in an attractive box or wrap them in cellophane tied with a colorful ribbon. You could even give a delicate cup and saucer packed with special cookies.

SOMETHING SPECIAL

Many of the cookies in this chapter are also wonderful accompaniments to creamy desserts and ice cream, adding a subtle but impressive flourish to any formal dinner party. And, of course, Amaretti, those crunchy, almond-flavored, moreish morsels from Italy, are traditionally served to guests with a glass of chilled white wine, whatever the time of day.

Allow a little more time for the recipes in this chapter, mainly because most of the cookies have extra decoration, so you will need time for them to cool and for frosting or melted chocolate to set. However, you are sure to find that this extra effort is worth it when you see how fast the cookies disappear from the plate.

MAKES 16
1½ sticks unsalted butter, plus extra
    for greasing
1½ cups all-purpose flour
1 tsp ground ginger
scant ½ cup golden superfine sugar

GINGER TOPPING
1 tbsp corn syrup
4 tbsp unsalted butter
2 tbsp confectioners' sugar
1 tsp ground ginger

WHITE FROSTING (OPTIONAL)
1¼ cups confectioners' sugar
1 tbsp milk

Ginger-Topped Fingers

The shortbread base will be quite soft when it first comes out of the oven, but it will become firm as it cools. These cookies are best left to cool completely before serving.

• Preheat the oven to 350°F/180°C. Grease a 11 x 7-inch/28 x 18-cm rectangular cake pan. Sift the flour and ginger into a bowl and stir in the sugar. Rub in the butter until the mixture resembles a dough.
• Press the mixture into the prepared pan and smooth the top with a spatula. Bake in the preheated oven for 40 minutes, or until very lightly browned.
• To make the ginger topping, place the syrup and butter in a small pan over low heat and stir until melted. Stir in the confectioners' sugar and ginger. Remove from the oven and pour over the topping while hot. Let cool slightly in the pan, then cut into 16 fingers. Transfer to cooling racks to cool completely.
• To make the frosting (if using), mix the confectioners' sugar with the milk until smooth. Pour it into a pastry bag with a thin tip, and pipe thin parallel lines lengthwise on top of each finger. Drag a cocktail stick or the tip of a knife crosswise through the lines, alternately toward you and then away from you, about ½ inch/1 cm apart, to create a wavy effect.

MAKES 12

1⅛ sticks unsalted butter, softened

¾ cup golden confectioners' sugar

scant 1 cup all-purpose flour

scant ½ cup unsweetened cocoa

½ tsp ground cinnamon

FILLING

4½ squares bittersweet chocolate,
    broken into pieces

scant ¼ cup heavy cream

Cookies and Cream Sandwiches

Do not sandwich the cookies together too long before serving, otherwise they will go soft. Store unsandwiched cookies in an airtight container for up to 3 days.

• Preheat the oven to 325°F/160°C. Line a cookie sheet with nonstick parchment paper. Place the butter and sugar in a large bowl and beat together until light and fluffy. Sift the flour, unsweetened cocoa, and ground cinnamon into the bowl and mix until a smooth dough forms.

• Place the dough between 2 sheets of nonstick parchment paper and roll out to ⅛ inch/3 mm thick. Stamp out 2½-inch/6-cm circles and place on the prepared cookie sheet. Bake in the preheated oven for 15 minutes, or until firm to the touch. Let cool for 2 minutes, then transfer to cooling racks to cool completely.

• To make the filling, place the chocolate and cream in a pan and heat gently until the chocolate has melted. Stir until smooth. Let cool, then let chill in the refrigerator for 2 hours, or until firm. Sandwich the cookies together in pairs with a spoonful of chocolate cream and serve.

MAKES ABOUT 40
1 cup blanched almonds
¾ cup superfine sugar
1 large egg white
confectioners' sugar, for dusting

Amaretti

To intensify the almond flavor, add a drop or two of almond extract with the egg white. This is the secret of the popular Amaretti di Saronno. You could also wrap individual cookies in colorful tissue paper if you are planning to give them as a gift.

• Preheat the oven to 250°F/120°C. Use a pestle and mortar to crush the almonds with the superfine sugar, or finely chop the almonds and then combine with the sugar in a bowl.

• Lightly beat the egg white, then stir it into the almond mixture to form a firm dough. Line 2 large cookie sheets with parchment paper and place walnut-sized portions of the dough on them, spaced well apart to allow for spreading. Dust with confectioners' sugar. Bake in the preheated oven for 30 minutes. Remove from the oven and transfer to cooling racks to cool.

MAKES 40
2 sticks unsalted butter, softened,
    plus extra for greasing
¼ cup golden superfine sugar
1½ cups all-purpose flour

scant 1 cup cornstarch
1 tsp ground cinnamon
½ cup sifted confectioners' sugar,
    to decorate

Mexican Pastelitos

These cookies are traditionally made in this small size, but you could make larger cookies, if you prefer.

• Preheat the oven to 325°F/160°C, then grease 2 cookie sheets. Place the butter and superfine sugar in a bowl and beat until light and fluffy. Sift the flour, cornstarch, and cinnamon into a separate bowl, then gradually work them into the creamed mixture with a wooden spoon. When well mixed, knead until smooth.

• Take 1 teaspoon at a time of the mixture and roll into a ball. Place the little balls on the prepared cookie sheets. Bake in the preheated oven for 30–40 minutes, or until pale golden.

• Place the confectioners' sugar in a shallow dish and toss the pastelitos in it while they are still warm. Let cool on cooling racks.

MAKES ABOUT 30

1 stick unsalted butter, softened,
    plus extra for greasing

½ cup golden confectioners' sugar,
    sifted

scant 1 cup all-purpose flour

1 tbsp unsweetened cocoa

3½ squares semisweet chocolate,
    melted and cooled

Chocolate Viennese Fingers

Sprinkle some chopped nuts onto the chocolate-coated ends of these cookies while the chocolate is still soft, if you like.

• Preheat the oven to 350°F/180°C. Grease 2 large cookie sheets. Beat the butter and sugar together until light and fluffy. Sift the flour and unsweetened cocoa into the bowl and work the mixture until it is a smooth consistency suitable for piping.

• Spoon into a large pastry bag fitted with a 1-inch/2.5-cm star tip. Pipe 2½-inch/6-cm lengths of the mixture onto the prepared cookie sheets, spacing them well apart to allow for spreading. Bake in the preheated oven for 15 minutes, or until firm.

• Remove from the oven and let cool on the cookie sheets for 2 minutes, then transfer to a cooling rack to cool completely. Dip the ends of the cookies into the melted chocolate and let set before serving.

MAKES 12

1⅜ sticks unsalted butter,
cut into small pieces,
plus extra for greasing

1½ cups all-purpose flour,
plus extra for dusting

generous ½ cup superfine sugar,
plus extra for dusting

1 tsp vanilla extract

Vanilla Hearts

Place a fresh vanilla bean in your superfine sugar and keep it in a storage jar for several weeks to give the sugar a delicious vanilla flavor.

• Preheat the oven to 350°F/180°C, then lightly grease a large cookie sheet. Sift the flour into a large bowl. Add the butter and rub in with your fingertips until the mixture resembles fine bread crumbs. Stir in the superfine sugar and vanilla extract and mix together to form a firm dough.

• Roll out the dough on a lightly floured counter to a thickness of 1 inch/2.5 cm. Stamp out 12 hearts with a heart-shaped cookie cutter measuring about 2 inches/5 cm across and 1 inch/2.5 cm deep. Arrange the hearts on the prepared cookie sheet.

• Transfer to the preheated oven and bake for 15–20 minutes, or until the hearts are a light golden color. Transfer the vanilla hearts to a cooling rack and let cool completely. Dust them with superfine sugar just before serving.

MAKES 12
4 tbsp unsalted butter,
    plus extra for greasing
⅓ cup raisins
2 tbsp brandy
4 squares bittersweet chocolate,
    broken into pieces
4 squares milk chocolate,
    broken into pieces

2 tbsp corn syrup
6 oz/175 g graham crackers,
    coarsely broken
½ cup slivered almonds,
    lightly toasted
scant ¼ cup candied cherries,
    chopped

TOPPING
3½ squares bittersweet chocolate,
    broken into pieces
scant 2 tbsp butter

Tiffin

For a decorative effect, use a fork to mark light wavy lines over the chocolate topping before leaving it to set in the refrigerator.

• Grease a 7-inch/18-cm shallow square cake pan and line the base with parchment paper. Place the raisins and brandy in a bowl and let soak for about 30 minutes. Put the chocolate, butter, and syrup in a pan and heat gently until melted.

• Stir in the graham crackers, almonds, cherries, raisins, and brandy. Turn the mixture into the prepared pan and let cool. Cover and let chill in the refrigerator for 1 hour.

• To make the topping, place the chocolate and butter in a small heatproof bowl and set over a pan of gently simmering water until melted. Stir and pour over the cookie base. Let chill in the refrigerator for 8 hours or overnight. Cut into bars or squares to serve.

MAKES 24

1½ sticks unsalted butter,
    plus extra for greasing

2 oz/55 g eating apple,
    cored and cooked

¼ cup soft brown sugar

5 tbsp molasses

1 egg white

1 tsp almond extract

1⅓ cups all-purpose flour

¼ tsp baking soda

¼ tsp baking powder

pinch of salt

½ tsp allspice

½ tsp ground ginger

Gingerbread Squares

Allspice is a mixture of various spices, but you could substitute your own combination of warming spices, such as ground cinnamon, freshly grated nutmeg or mace, and ground cloves.

• Preheat the oven to 350°F/180°C. Grease a large cake pan and line it with parchment paper. Chop the apple and set aside. Put the butter, sugar, molasses, egg white, and almond extract in a food processor and process until the mixture is smooth.

• Sift together the flour, baking soda, baking powder, salt, allspice, and ginger in another bowl. Add to the creamed mixture and beat together well until combined. Stir the apple into the mixture, then pour the mixture into the prepared cake pan.

• Transfer to the preheated oven and bake for 10 minutes, or until golden brown. Remove from the oven and cut into 24 pieces. Transfer the gingerbread to a cooling rack and let cool completely before serving.

MAKES 20

1¼ sticks unsalted butter

generous ½ cup superfine sugar

1 egg yolk

generous 1 cup ground almonds

generous 1 cup all-purpose flour

2 squares semisweet chocolate,
  broken into pieces

2 tbsp confectioners' sugar

2 tbsp unsweetened cocoa

Ladies' Kisses

Place the dough balls well apart from each other on the cookie sheets because they will spread out during cooking. You may need to bake the cookies in batches.

• Line 3 cookie sheets with parchment paper or use nonstick sheets. Beat the butter and superfine sugar together in a bowl until pale and fluffy. Beat in the egg yolk, then the almonds and flour. Continue beating until well mixed. Shape the dough into a ball, then wrap in plastic wrap and let chill in the refrigerator for 1½–2 hours.

• Preheat the oven to 325°F/160°C. Unwrap the dough and break off walnut-size pieces, then roll them into balls between the palms of your hands. Place the dough balls on the prepared cookie sheets, spaced well apart to allow for spreading. Bake in the preheated oven for 20–25 minutes, or until golden brown. Remove from the oven and carefully transfer the cookies, still on the parchment paper if using, to cooling racks to cool.

• Place the chocolate in a small heatproof bowl set over a pan of gently simmering water, and stir constantly until melted. Remove the bowl from the heat. Remove the cookies from the parchment paper, if using, and spread the melted chocolate over the bases. Sandwich them together in pairs and return to the cooling racks to cool and set. Dust with a mixture of sifted confectioners' sugar and cocoa and serve.

MAKES 12

1 stick unsalted butter, softened,
    plus extra for greasing

¼ cup golden superfine sugar,
    plus extra for dusting

1 tsp chopped lavender leaves

finely grated rind of 1 lemon

generous 1 cup all-purpose flour

Lavender Cookies

If you do not have a food processor, you can mix the dough by hand. Knead it into a ball before rolling the dough out.

• Preheat the oven to 300°F/150°C, then grease a large cookie sheet. Place the superfine sugar and lavender leaves in a food processor. Process until the lavender is very finely chopped, then add the butter and lemon rind and continue to process until light and fluffy. Transfer to a large bowl. Sift in the flour and beat until the mixture forms a stiff dough.

• Place the dough on a sheet of parchment paper and place another sheet on top. Gently press down with a rolling pin and roll out to ⅛–¼ inch/3–5 mm thick. Remove the top sheet of paper and stamp out circles from the dough using a 2¾-inch/7-cm round cookie cutter. Re-knead and re-roll the trimmings and stamp out more cookies.

• Using a spatula, transfer the cookies to the prepared cookie sheet. Prick them with a fork and bake in the preheated oven for 12 minutes, or until pale brown. Remove from the oven and cool on the cookie sheet for 2 minutes, then transfer to a cooling rack to cool completely.

Index